101 Questions
About
Cataract Surgery

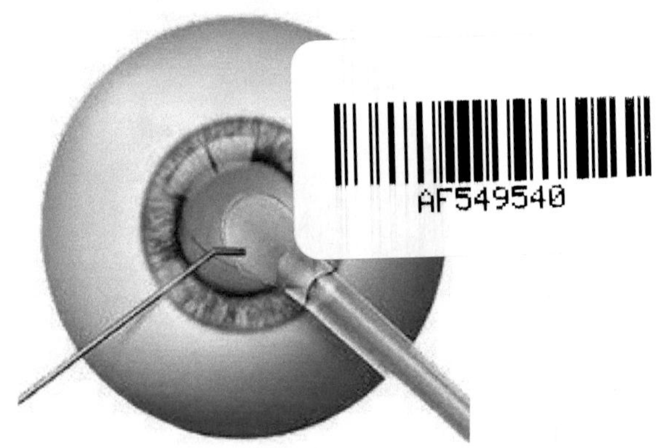

Dr. P. B. Sarkar

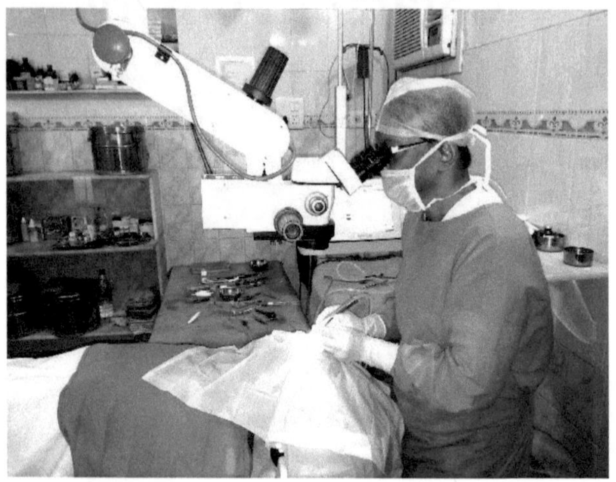

Cataract Phaco surgery performed by the Author

Those who fear Cataract Surgery

First Edition May 2023

Published by

Salt Lake Eye Foundation

Introduction

According to a recent report, published by The World Health Organization (WHO), more than 18 million people are bilaterally blind from cataracts in the world. This means almost half of all global cases of blindness is due to cataract. Cataract remains the leading cause of blindness and is an important cause of visual impairment across the globe. Fortunately, a major portion of this blindness is reversible, if surgical interventions are done in time.

In cataracts, the transparent lens inside the eye, termed the 'Crystalline lens' becomes cloudy or opaque and obstructs the vision. In surgery, the cataract is removed and replaced with an artificial lens (called an intraocular lens or IOL) to restore clear vision. The procedure typically is performed on an outpatient basis and does not require any overnight stay in a hospital or other care facility.

Most modern surgical procedures of cataract management involve the use of a high-frequency ultrasound device that breaks up the cloudy lens into small pieces, which are then gently removed from the eye with the help of a

Phaco machine.

Nowadays Cataract surgery is safe, quick, and painless procedure resulting in excellent visual outcomes and almost no or very minimal complications.

Still, many people suffer from some fear of surgery. Moreover, they have lot of questions about cataracts, especially their safety and after results. In this book, I have answered 101 such common questions about cataracts, their surgical overview, investigation details, after-operation care, probable complications, the cost factor, and many more.

Hope the discussions in this book will be helpful to them.

Dr Purnendu Bikash Sarkar
Kolkata, March 2023
Email : pbsarkar@gmail.com

Contents

The Cataract 8

Phaco surgery Error! Bookmark not defined.

Intra Ocular Lens 31

Monofocal IOL 34

Multifocal IOL 35

Investigations 36

Expenditure 40

Follow up 44

Complications 46

Take Home Massage 48

ABOUT THE COMPILER 49

The Cataract

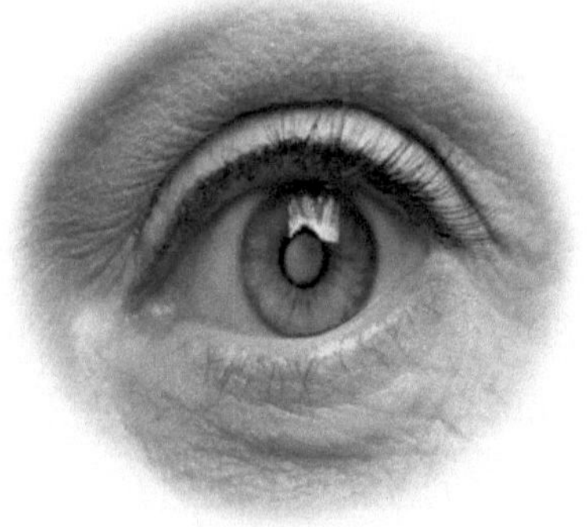

What is Cataract?

Cataract is the clouding of the natural lens of human eyes. It is the most common cause of vision loss in people over age 40 and is also the principal cause of blindness in the world. Blindness due to cataract is reversible if the surgery done in proper time.

What is the cause of Cataract?

Age is the main cause of cataract formation. Injury to the eye, some medicines like Steroids, excessive exposure to sunlight, smoking, genetic factors, diabetes, etc. are the other causes. Cataracts can also be seen in newborn babies called Congenital cataract. Recent studies have shown that people who live in high altitudes are more at risk of developing cataracts.

What are the Symptoms of Cataracts?

Symptoms of cataracts are cloudy vision, problems reading in low light, a halo around a light, driving discomfort, frequent change of glass power, etc. are the main symptoms of cataracts. It may also be associated with double vision, watering from the eyes, colour vision defects, and eye strain. Usually, cataract is a painless disease.

What is the age of Cataract formation?

Cataracts can develop at any age, even in childhood. But according to recent studies, the average age is considered 65 years. In 2004, the average age was around 73 to 75 years.

All cataracts are of the same type?

No, basically, there are three different types of cataracts.

- Primary or age-related cataracts. Also called a nuclear cataract (effected the central portion of the lens).
- Cortical cataract that affects the peripheral portion of the lens.
- Subscapular cataract (affecting the capsule of the lens). As a person ages, any one type, or a combination of any of these three types, can develop over time.

What is the treatment of cataracts?

Phaco surgery with Implantation of an Intra-Ocular Lens (IOL) inside the eye is the most modern treatment procedure for cataracts. Earlier procedures like ICCE, ECCE, SICS, etc. have become obsolete due to their long recovery period, poor results, unhappy post-operative vision, and many complications.

Can I remove my cataract with eye drops?

Unfortunately, NO. Surgery is the only way to cure cataracts. But some research centers are exploring another approach to treatment. They are trying to invent eye drops that may dissolve cataracts so that patients do not have to go to surgery in the future.

Can I see my cataract in the mirror?

The natural crystalline lens in our eyes is colorless and transparent. A cataract is the clouding of this colorless Lens. Over time it changes to a brownish or yellowish hue. Other people can easily see this change of colour from outside. Yes, you can self-assess yourself with the help of a mirror.

Can spectacles improve poor vision due to cataract?

While prescription glasses cannot directly treat or cure cataracts. In some early cases, poor vision due to cataracts can marginally be improved by changing the glass power. Incising light over the reading object and in the room can give some relief. In certain types of cataracts, using dark glasses in the outdoors can help better vision. But all these are totally temporary and very soon vision deteriorates again.

Even with a cataract how some people can read books?

A cataract is basically the hardening and clouding of the clear crystalline lens of our eye. This is usually an aging process. As the lens becomes opaque, its refractive index changes which make it possible to focus light rays on the retina. This refractive mechanism helps people read books even with cataracts. So sometimes in cataract people can read books without spectacle. Many people call this as 'New vision'.

Can cataracts vanish automatically?

A cataract is the hardening of the natural clear lens of the eye. It is a one-way physiological procedure. Cataract increases and becomes more advance with age, but do not go back to their previous condition automatically. In the case of cataracts due to diabetes, vision improves if the blood sugar level is reduced.

Is there any Natural Cure for Cataracts?

There is no natural cure for cataracts. There is no way to prevent cataract formation or slow its progression. But some healthy lifestyle practices may be helpful.

- Regular eye examinations can detect and treat eye problems earlier.

- Stop smoking, reduce alcohol consumption, and treat health problems like diabetes, hypertension, high blood cholesterol, etc.
- Eat fruits and vegetables. A diet rich in vitamins and minerals and antioxidants can reduce the risk of developing cataracts.
- Wear sunglasses at outdoors. Ultraviolet light exposure may contribute to the development of cataracts.
- Some medicines enhance cataract formation. Ask your doctor if they can be avoid or reduce the doses.

What is the best technique for cataract operation?

Phaco surgery with the Implantation of an Intra Ocular lens (IOL) inside the eye is the most modern and safe procedure to get rid of cataracts.

What is the best time for a cataract operation?

When it becomes difficult to watch TV, read a book, or drive a car, consider the operation of your cataract. Nowadays, with technical advances and safety, people like to get relief from their cataracts early. In the case of advanced mature cataracts, the operation must be done as early as possible. Still, early surgery gives the best result.

How serious is a cataract operation?

All surgery carries some risk factor. Fortunately, with better machines, surgical techniques and the availability of excellent Intra Ocular Lenses (IOL), cataract surgery is highly safe and successful nowadays. And the success rate is approximately 98%. Still, there remains the risk of some potential complications, which sometimes become serious. Pain after the operation, infection of the eye, redness, or even permanent loss of vision may result in grave disappointment after cataract surgery.

Is cataract surgery done by injection?

Even a few years back, for anesthesia during cataract operations, surgeons used to inject xylocaine (an anesthetic solution) around the eyeball. These caused apprehension and pain in the eyes. But in modern surgeries, most cataract operations are done by using only eye drops like proparacaine. This is called Topical Anesthesia. No injections are needed.

Is a Cataract operation painful?

Cataract operation if done under Topical anesthesia (by using eye drops) is almost painless, though somebody feels some mild discomfort during surgery.

How long do I have to stay on OT for Phaco surgery?

Phaco surgery is a quick procedure. A skilled surgeon usually takes 10 to 15 minutes time to finish the operation. But in case of unfortunate complications like rupture of the posterior capsule, lens drop, increased Intra Ocular Pressure, etc. the surgical time may extend up to one hour or more.

Shall I remain awake during surgery?

Yes, you will remain awake during cataract surgery. You may feel slight discomfort which is well tolerable. You can hear your favorite music or even talk with the surgical team members to reduce your tension and anxiety.

What will happen if I blink during the operation?

Anesthetic eye drops are applied to your eyes prior to surgery to make the procedure comfortable and decrease your natural urge to blink. Also, a small device (speculum) will hold your eyelids open during the procedure, so you can't accidentally blink and your eyelids cannot interfere with any step of the surgery

When shall I be released from the Hospital?
Phaco surgery is done as an outdoor procedure. Like in earlier days, now patients do not have to stay overnight in the hospital. So, if no complications arise, usually half an hour after surgery you should be released from the Hospital.

Do I need to wear sunglass after surgery?
Yes, you must have to wear sunglass at least for one week after surgery to prevent infection, injury, dust, ultraviolet rays, and glare from bright light. The sunglass must be of good quality to prevent ultraviolet rays enter into the eye.

Can I watch TV after the operation?
After the first day of surgery, you can watch TV, do a computer, and read a book. But don't rub the operated eye. Using a protective dark glass for at least seven days and wearing an eye shield during sleep prevents many accidental injuries and infections after the operation.

Can I take shower after the operation?
After uneventful cataract surgery the next day you can take shower, but avoid direct water in the eye for 7 days. Better to avoid cooking for a

week to prevent infection.

Shall I have to apply eye drops after the operation?

Yes, as per your doctor's advice, you must have to apply some eye drops regularly to prevent infection and other complications, which helps early recovery and excellent vision.

What I can eat after the operation?

You can eat and drink anything you like, but should not be too spicy. It must not upset your digestive system. Take your normal medicines as before. It is better to avoid smoking and minimize alcohol intake.

Can I sleep on the operated side?

For the first day don't sleep on the operated side. From the next day, you can sleep as you like but never face down.

May I have to use an eye shield?

For the first few days after the operation wearing an eye shield during sleep is good to protect the operated eye from accidental injury. Clean the eye shield properly before use. It must not be loosely fitted on your face.

When can I use my mobile or laptop?
Day after the operation you can use all digital gadgets like smartphones, laptops, iPad, etc. But if you feel tiredness in the eyes, headache, or watering from the eyes, be away from the gadgets.

Can I use my old spectacle after the operation?
After the operation, usually the power of your old spectacle changes. In most cases, glass power reduces and becomes almost normal. But it takes some time to settle the final power. Till then you can use your old spectacle (if it is not of thick glass) temporarily. It will not harm, but it may cause blurred vision or even eye pain.

When I can drive my car after the operation?
Seven days after the operation you can drive your car. But avoid public transport for the first few days. If only one eye is operated be careful during driving.

What is the best season for cataract surgery?
In earlier days, because of the prolonged recovery period, patients preferred the winter season for cataract surgery. Nowadays all seasons are safe for cataract operation.

Shall I get back my good vision after surgery?

If there is no serious disease in the eye, you should get back the beautiful childhood vision after surgery. But in case of any preexisting eye disease like glaucoma, macular degeneration, diabetic retinopathy, etc. your vision may not be satisfactory even after an excellent and uncomplicated operation.

Is it possible to presume my post-portative vision?

Yes, there are many methods and investigations to get an idea of your post-operative vision. That includes a thorough examination of the retina after dilatation of the pupil, perimeter, OCT, DFA, USG, etc.

After surgery when shall I get back my vision?

Usually next day after operation your vision improves a lot. You can watch TV or see near objects or even read books. With time vision improves gradually and within 2 to 3 weeks you will get excellent vision. In some cases, new spectacle power is prescribed 3 weeks after the operation.

What is the lifetime of an implanted IOL?

The IOLs implanted in the eyes usually last till the death of the person. There is no wear and tear or maintenance of the implanted IOL.

Shall I have to wear a spectacle after the operation?

In the case of a Monofocal IOL implant, you may need slight power in your spectacle for crystal clear and sharp vision. On the other hand, in the case of Multifocal or Progressive IOL, you will be able to see everything, even read without any spectacle.

What I must not do after surgery?

- Don't drive a car at least for one week.
- Don't do any heavy lifting or strenuous activity for a few weeks.
- Immediately after the procedure, avoid bending over to prevent putting extra pressure on your eye.
- Don’t rub your eyes
- Avoid water in the operated eye for one week.
- Better to avoid smoking.
- Avoid crowdy, windy, or dusty area.

Does the cataract come back again after the operation?

Once a cataract is removed, it does not grow back. However, a clear membrane is left behind the IOL at the time of surgery. Over time, this membrane may become hazy causing decreased vision and increased glare to light. This is called Posterior Capsule Opacification. A simple laser application can clean the opacification within moments.

Can I smoke or drink alcohol after operation?

It is better to avoid smoking and alcohol consumption for a few weeks after cataract surgery. Smoking causes dryness of the eyes which hampers normal post-operative recovery. Alcohol can increase blood sugar levels leading to damage to the retina.

Can I brush my tooth and wash my face after the operation?

You can gently brush your tooth. Before that Wash your hands thoroughly with soap and water and dry them with a clean towel. If you want to shave be careful of entering the water into the eye.

Does cataract surgery improve night vision?

Yes, cataract surgery will improve your night vision for driving, walking, and any other activities even in low light. Removing your cataract and replacing it with a crystal-clear intraocular lens (IOL) typically will result in a dramatic improvement in the clarity and quality of your vision.

Dressing of the operated eye

- *Wash your hands thoroughly with soap and water and dry them with a clean towel. Don't use any hand sanitizer.*
- *Carefully remove the eye pad from the eye.*
- *Use boiled water and cool it (distilled water) to clean the operated eye.*
- *Dip some cotton balls or gauze pieces in this water and gently clean the margins of the eyelids.*
- *Put the eye drops as directed by the doctor. One drop is enough.*
- *Put on the dark glass.*
- *At bedtime cover the eye with a protective shield.*

Phaco surgery

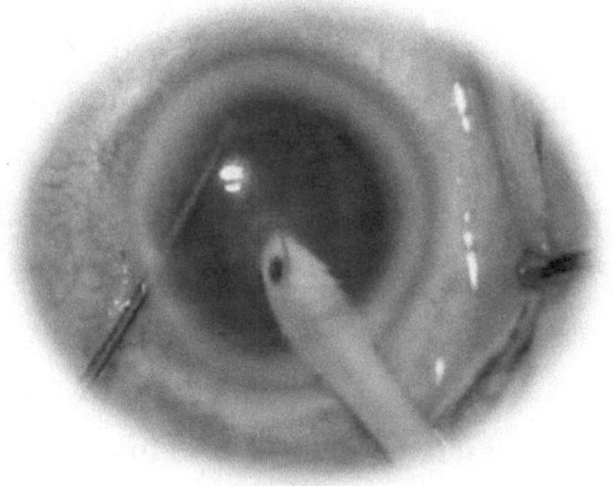

What are the types of cataract surgery?

Basically, two types of operation are done to remove cataract. The Most popular one is Phaco surgery. In this technique, a small corneal incision, less than 2 mm is done on the cornea. The other one is ECCE (Extra Capsular Cataract Extraction) where a large incision or cut is made on the cornea to remove the cataract. In this case, several stitches are necessary to close the wound. Another procedure called ICCE (Intra Capsular Cataract Extraction) was popular in the older days, where after making a very large cut in the cornea surgeons removed the whole cataract with forceps. In ICCE patients had to use a very thick spectacle for vision. This technique is obsolete nowadays.

What is the Phaco surgery procedure?

Phaco surgery, full-form Phacoemulsification cataract surgery, is a procedure where an ultrasonic device is used to break and remove the cataract or opaque lens from the eye through a very small corneal incision. After removal of the cataract, almost in all cases, an Intraocular lens (IOL) is implanted into the eye to improve vision.

Phaco surgery or ECCE which is better for me?

Phaco surgery is definitely better. It is safe, almost hazardless, quick recovery, excellent vision quality, and with any or minimal complication. On the other hand, ECCE carries some risk of infection, takes long time for recovery and patient have to follow many restrictions. Also vision quality is not as good as Phaco surgery, and needs more glass power.

Is Phaco surgery safe for me?

With modern phaco-machines, better phaco-dynamics and IOL phacoemulsification surgery is safe and effective for patients suffering from cataracts. It gives fast recovery, excellent visual outcome, early mobilization, and less or no complication.

Why is Phaco surgery safe?

Compared to ECCE or ICCE Phaco surgery is very safe because the operation is done through a small less than 2mm cut in the cornea. So, the chance of infection, bleeding, etc. is minimal. Moreover, surgical time is very short and quick recovery.

What is laser Phaco surgery?

Traditional Phaco surgery is done with the help of ultrasound energy. But this can be done by laser-ray also. In Laser cataract surgeries, instead of a hand-held blade, a beam of laser rays is used to break up and remove cataracts followed by the implantation of IOL.

Is laser surgery better than traditional Phaco surgery?

Laser Phaco surgery does not require any blade, it increases accuracy, and precision and reduces surgical time. But at the end of the day the, visual outcome is almost the same in both types of surgeries.

Is laser Phaco surgery expensive?

The surgical cost of laser Phaco surgery is much higher than traditional Phaco surgery. Cost depends from center to center.

Can Phaco surgery correct astigmatism?

Astigmatism is a condition where the shape of the cornea is slightly oblique, not spherical on all sides. This can be corrected during cataract surgery by implanting a Toric IOL. These are a special type of customized IOL. The best results depend on accurate pre-operative refraction, biometry, and some other factors. Using an appropriate Toric IOL, astigmatism can also be corrected the by Phaco surgery technique.

During the operation shall the surgeon put stitches in my eye?

Phaco surgery is done through a less than 2mm incision in the cornea of your eye. The surgeon does not put any stitches in this small incision. But in the case of ECCE operation stitches are necessary to close the incision wound.

How long it takes to complete a cataract operation?

That depends on the surgeon's experience and the quality and specification of the phaco-machine. In an uncomplicated cataract, a skilled surgeon can finish the operation in less than 10 minutes. The time duration also depends on the type of cataract and its hardness, cooperation of the patient and speed of the OT staffs.

Shall I feel any pain during surgery?

Cataract surgery is basically done by anesthetic eye drops, no injection in the eyes are needed. During surgery you may feel mild and tolerable discomfort. You may see various colours in front of your eye. Usually there is no pain but you may feel slight pressure on the eye during the implantation of the IOL.

What shall I feel after surgery?

After surgery, you will be relaxed and tension-free. In case of pain, your doctor may prescribe a painkiller tablet. Your operated eye will remain closed by a protective cover. You will walk out from the operating theatre and take rest for some time in bed. Shortly you may be released to go home.

Can both eyes be operated at the same sitting?

Usually, cataracts of both eyes are not operated at the same sittings. Sometimes that may cause severe complications. It is better to be done at least after 1 week. But in case of emergency, some surgeons prefer to operate at the same sitting.

Can Phaco surgery give 100% guarantee of my vision?

No. Any surgery on human body cannot give 100% guarantee of success. But in modern Phaco surgery done by advanced computerised phaco-machines, availability of better IOL, medicines and experience surgeon, success rate is over 99%. Please note patient also have a great role in the success of cataract surgery. They must follow the directions and safety measures advised by the doctor.

On which factor success of surgery depends?

An experienced and well trained surgeon, advanced and good phaco-machine with an excellent phaco-dynamic facility, better IOL quality, sterile and well-equipped operation theatre, trained OT staff, proper post-operative care, patient's personal hygiene, are the key points of a successful phaco-operation. Moreover, unnecessary delay in taking a decision for operation by the patient may lead to the hardening of cataracts, leading to post-operative unhappy vision.

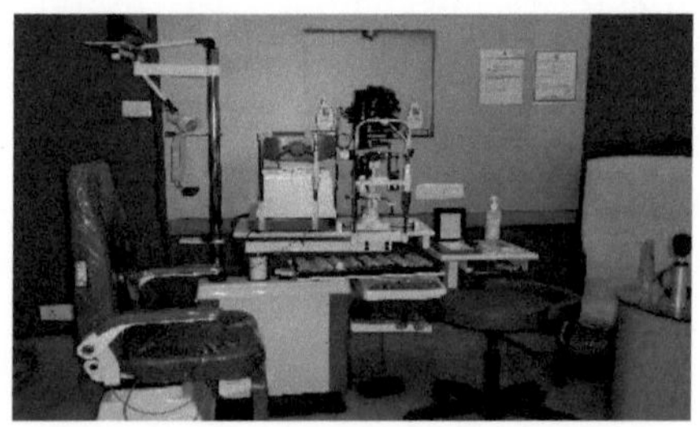

Salt Lake Eye Foundation

Intra Ocular Lens
IOL

What is an IOL?

The full form of IOL is Intra Ocular Lens. After cataract operation your surgeon will implant an artificial lens in your eyes, so that you can see properly after operation.

By which material IOL is made of?

IOLs are artificial lens. They are circular in shape, biconvex, crystal clear and transparent. These are made of glass, synthetic materials, silicon, etc. Glass IOLs are hard or rigid. IOLs made of synthetic plastic or silicon are soft and malleable. These IOLs can be folded and are easy to insert in the eye through a small incision or cut on the cornea

What are the types of IOL?

There are basically two types of IOL. Monofocal and Multifocal. In monofocal IOL, there is only a single focus point, and after the operation patients have to wear a spectacle for clear vision, both distant and near. Multifocal IOL contains a series of lenses of different power. These are called 'Lens Corridors'. So, after the operation, patients need no spectacle and they get full freedom of vision at every distance without spectacles.

Is it mandatory to implant an IOL into my eye?

The implant of an IOL into the eye after the removal of cataracts gives sharp and clear post-operative vision. Otherwise, you may need thick and heavy glass to see, which is very uncomfortable and inconvenient. And it is also obsolete nowadays.

Which type of IOL is most popular?

Monofocal IOLs are the most widely used in cataract phaco surgery. These types of IOLs are designed to give you crisp, clear vision at one particular distance. Compared to Multifocal, Monofocal IOL is less expensive. In monofocal IOL spectacles are necessary to see everything clearly.

Which IOL is best for me?

That depends on your activity, age, condition of cataract, any underlying eye disease, brand, and budget. Your doctor may guide you properly. But you must understand clearly about advantages and disadvantages of both types of IOLs.

Monofocal vs Multifocal IOL

Monofocal IOL

Advantages of Monfocal IOL:

- *Monofocal IOL gives better vision in low light than Multicocal IOL.*
- *In case of astigmatic eye, Monofocal IOL is the best choice. These lenses are called Toric IOL. They improve vision much better. Multicocal IOL can not give satisfactory vision in an astigmatic eye.*

Disadvantages of Monofocal lenses*:*

- *In cases of Monofocal IOL, patients have to use spectacle either for near or distant vision or both. Without spectacle, the patient cannot enjoy fully satisfactory vision.*
- *In the case of astigmatism standard Monfocal IOL, cause blurred vision, and the patient still suffers from short-sightedness or long-sightedness*

Multifocal IOL

This type of lens will allow you to see all ranges of vision near, intermediate, and far. The lenses work by using several different optical powers at varying points across the lens. These work best if they are implanted into both the eyes.

Advantages of multifocal IOL:

- *In the case of a Multifocal IOL implant, about 95 percent of patients no longer need to wear glasses for their regular activities.*
- *Multifocal lenses can often offer excellent distance and near vision, meaning that if you work at a computer all day, it could be the perfect choice for you.*

Disadvantages of multifocal lenses:

- *About 10 percent of patients who have used Multifocal IOLs suffer from halo or glare when looking towards lights at night. However, many patients do adapt to this after a short period of time.*
- *A small proportion of patients, may need a lower power reading glass when looking at very fine print such as medicine bottles.*

Pre-Operative

Investigations

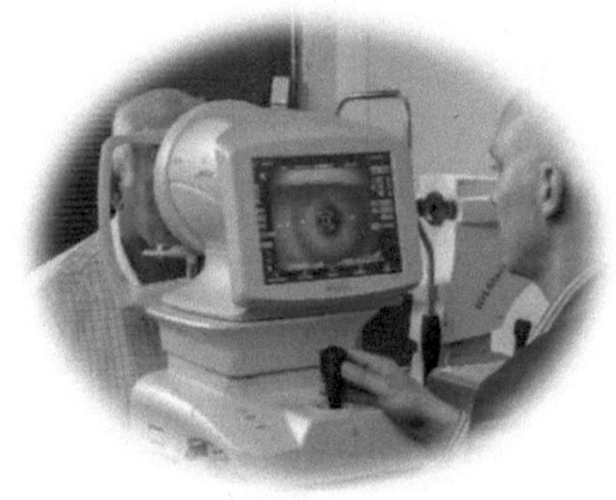

Which Investigations are necessary before cataract operation?

A thorough and series eye checkup is done for evaluation of acuity of vision, condition of retina, any other eye problems, type and maturity of cataract etc. Other investigations are Biometry, OCT, Specular Microscopy, Ultra-sonogram, Blood sugar, Cardiac checkup, Blood pressure, Eye pressure (IOP), Perimetry, Gonioscopy, etc.

What is Biometry?

Biometry is the calculation of power of the Intra Ocular Lens which will be implanted into the eye during surgery. In a cataract operation, Biometry is the most important issue because the visual outcome and success of the operation depend on the accuracy of biometry.

What is OCT

OCT, full from Optical coherence tomography, is an imaging method used to generate a picture of the back of your eye, called Retina. This non-invasive method detects the health of the retina and gives an idea about the after-operation visual improvement.

What is Specular Microscopy?

The specular microscope is a valuable tool to evaluate the corneal endothelium cell count and function and functional reserve of the cornea. This is also an invasive procedure.

Why Ultrasonogram of the eye is necessary?

USG or an Ultrasonogram of the eye gives a detailed picture of the inner portion of the eye. It detects any blood clots or debris in the vitreous, position of the cataractous lens, the health of the retina, and so on.

Can diabetic patients go for cataract surgery?

Diabetes causes cataracts and many patients seeking surgery have coexisting diabetes. Surgery is performed when their blood sugar label is well controlled. But if there is any retinal problem like diabetic retinopathy, macular edema, or retinal hemorrhage, those must be treated before the operation.

What blood sugar is safe for cataract operation?

A well-controlled blood sugar is always good and safe for cataract operation. Phaco surgery can be done safely with post-prandial blood sugar within 180 mg/dl. But the most important factor is HbA1c label, which is considered safe if its value is less than 6.

Shall I have to control my blood pressure?

Definitely. High blood pressure may cause many complications during surgery like a stony eye, bleeding in the eye resulting in failure to implant the IOL, and even blindness. Safe blood pressure level is 130/80 mm of Hg.

What other physical conditions must be checked before surgery?

In the case of asthma blood carbon dioxide percentage should be checked. History of any medicine allergy, heart function, prostate in adult males, rheumatism, kidney function, etc. must be investigated before surgery.

Shall I have to check my tooth problems?

Any infectious condition of your tooth can cause serious complications after an operation. You need healthy teeth and good oral hygiene.

Expenditure

What is the cost of cataract surgery?

Cost of cataract surgery depends on the type of surgery like, ECCE, SICS or Phaco surgery, type and brand of the IOL, whether it is Imported or not, Monfocal or Multifocal, the property of the IOL, etc. Cost also depends on the tariffs of hospitals, Nursing Homes, and private clinics. Also, doctor's fee varies from surgeon to surgeon.

What is the average cost of Phaco surgery in India?

The average cost of Phaco surgery in India is between 10000 to 98000 in private hospitals, private clinics, and non-government centers. The cost also varies from surgeon to surgeon, state to state, etc. In government hospitals, the cost is much less than in private organizations.

Is Multifocal IOL expensive?

Multifocal IOLs are more expensive compared to monofocal IOL. The cost of Toric IOL is much higher than the average Monfocal.

Scope of low-cost surgery

Many charitable institutions, private clinics, corporate hospitals, and government hospitals have charitable wings to give service for economically poor patients. They offer low-cost cataract surgery

Does my medical insurance cover cataract surgery?

Most insurance companies cover expenditures for cataract operation. But there are some definite terms and conditions like a minimum lock-period, premium status, duration of cataract, and relation of cataract with other diseases. Please ask your insurance agent for detail.

Can I get a cashless facility?

Yes. You can enjoy a cashless facility for your cataract operation through your TPA. But you have to submit all valid documents and fulfill other T&C.

What documentation is necessary for cashless Phaco surgery through medical insurance?

In India, you need to submit current and previous 2-year policy copies, copies of your TPA photo cards, ID proof like Aadhar card, passport photograph, doctor's prescription with biometry report, investigation reports, etc.

How much money shall I get from medical insurance?

In India, earlier insurance companies used to pay the full bill submitted by the patient. Now there are definite slabs for the sanctioned amount. That depends upon the insurance company, their TPA, policy criteria, etc.

Shall I have to pay extra if I opt for a better IOL?

Yes, you can choose a better IOL over your sanctioned amount. In that case, you have to deposit the balance money which you cannot claim from the insurance company as reimbursement.

In medical insurance, can I go for reimbursement?

Definitely, you can opt for reimbursement. In that case, you have to send a prior intimation to your insurance company before surgery. And, after surgery submit all medical bills, money receipts, IOL packet with an ID card, doctor's prescriptions, etc. along with a claim form to the concerned insured company.

Follow up

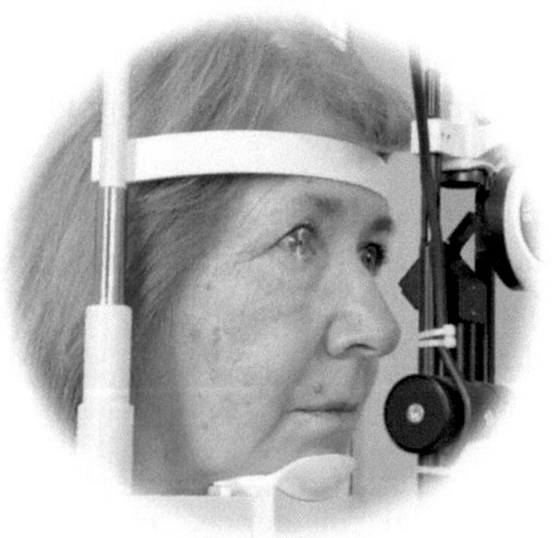

After operation when shall I consult my doctor first?

Usually day after operation you have to visit your doctor for a checkup. This first checkup is most important for the smooth recovery of your eye. Your doctor will examine the position of IOL, any sign of inflammation or infection, the state of the cornea, and the improvement of vision. He also adjusts the medication doses as required.

Do I need any further checkups?

Two to three weeks after the operation your doctor will again examine your eye and if everything is OK, he will prescribe your glass power, if needed. It is better to have a final check, a few months after the surgery

In which condition I must visit my doctor urgently?

After the operation in case of any pain in the eye, watering, redness, discharge, fall of vision, headache, etc. you must rush to your doctor without delay. These may be signs of serious complications.

Complications

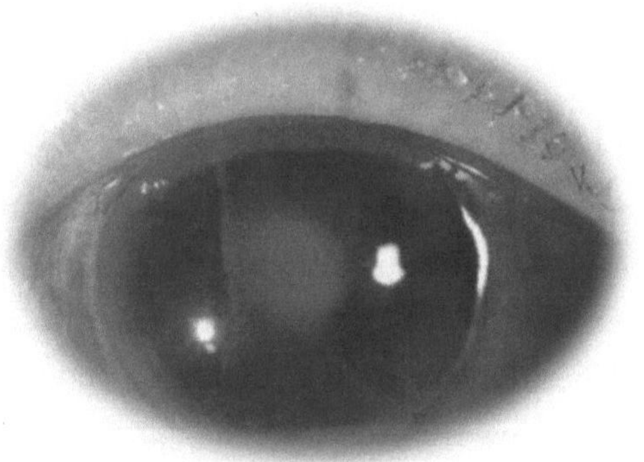

Is there any risk of Cataract surgery?

Yes. Few complications may occur after operation like posterior capsule opacity, dislocation of IOL, eye infection, increased light sensitivity, macular edema, and drooping of the eyelid. But don't be afraid, these complications are very rare. And early management can solve many of these complications

- Posterior capsule opacity (PCO)
- Intraocular lens dislocation
- Eye inflammation
- Light sensitivity
- Photopsia (perceived flashes of light)
- Macular edema (swelling of the central retina)
- Ptosis (droopy eyelid)
- Ocular hypertension (elevated eye pressure)
- Endophthalmitis (severe eye infection)
- Blindness

Take Home Massage

With the advancement of a modern approach to cataract surgery, high-end Phaco-Machine, Intra Ocular Lens, OT environment, and Medicines, cataract surgery is now very safe and rewarding.

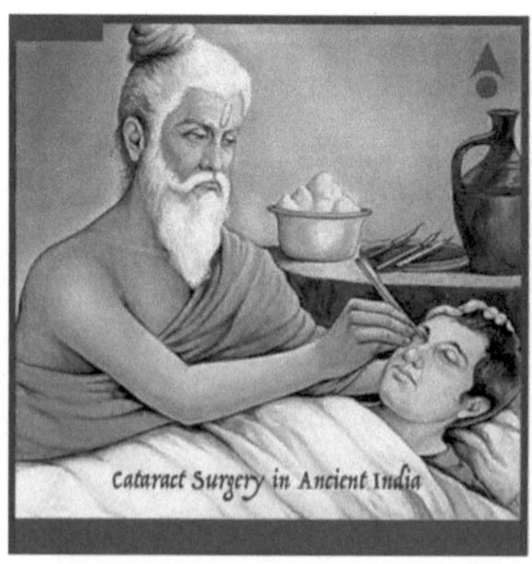
Cataract Surgery in Ancient India

ABOUT THE COMPILER

Dr. Purnendu Bikash Sarkar is a renowned Ophthalmologist. In his long career, Dr. Sarkar performed around one lakh cataract surgeries and treated innumerable patients suffering from various eye ailments. Dr. Sarkar loves to conduct eye camps, seminars, workshops, etc. to make people aware of various eye diseases. He has published numerous books and articles on his subject in peer-reviewed journals.

As an ardent Tagore lover and researcher, Dr. Sarkar has digitally compiled all songs and poems penned by Rabindranath Tagore, in two wonderful interactive software programs, **Gitabitan Archive** and **Rabindra Kobita Archive.**

Other Books of this Author

Gitabitan Thtyabhandar
Rabindra Ganer Antarale
Ruper Arale
Dinguli Tnar
Chokher Katha
Chasmar Handbook
Gatewat to Happy Vision
250 Rabindra Sangeet translated by Tagore in English

e-Books: Available in Amazon KDP

Song Offerings English Gitanjali
46 Rabindra Sangeet
101 Questions about Cataract Surgery
Handbook of Spectacle
103 Recitations of English Gitanjali

Purnendu Bikash Sarkar
pbsarkar@gmail.com

9 798890 260703

Printed by Libri Plureos GmbH in Hamburg, Germany